MODERN STARS

TAYLOR SWIFT

by Liz Sonneborn

Essential Library

An Imprint of Abdo Publishing

abdobooks.com

ABDOBOOKS.COM

Published by Abdo Publishing, a division of ABDO, PO Box 398166, Minneapolis, Minnesota 55439.

Printed in China.
102025
012026

Cover Photo: John Shearer/Getty Images for The Recording Academy/Getty Images Entertainment/Getty Images
Interior Photos: Valerie Macon/AFP/Getty Images, 5; Lisa Maree Williams/Getty Images, 8, 92; Jameis Delaynee/Alamy, 11; Allen J. Schaben/Los Angeles Times/Getty Images, 12; Jeremy Drey/MediaNews Group/Reading Eagle/Getty Images, 15; Tim Mosenfelder/Archive Photos/Getty Images, 17; Jesse D. Garrabrant/NBAE/NBA Classic/Getty Images, 18; Robert Alexander/Archive Photos/Getty Images, 20; Al Messerschmidt/Getty Images, 22–23; Frazer Harrison/ACM2009/Getty Images, 24; Kevin Winter/ACMA/Getty Images, 27; Jeff Kravitz/FilmMagic, Inc/Getty Images, 29, 33, 35; Kevin Mazur/WireImage/Getty Images, 37, 56, 61; Larry Busacca/Getty Images Entertainment/Getty Images, 40; Jim Ruymen/UPI/Alamy, 43; Hubert Boesl/dpa picture alliance/Alamy, 45; Kevin Mazur/WireImage for MTV/WireImage/Getty Images, 48; Walden Media/Album/Alamy, 51; Jeff Kravitz/AMA2011/FilmMagic, Inc/Getty Images, 54; Frederick M. Brown/Getty Images Entertainment/Getty Images, 59; Jackson Lee/GC Images/Getty Images, 64; Theo Stroomer/Getty Images Entertainment/Getty Images, 66; Mpi04/Media Punch Inc/Alamy Live News/Alamy, 69; Christian Bertrand/Shutterstock Images, 72; Lester Cohen/Getty Images for Universal Music Group/Getty Images Entertainment/Getty Images, 75; Kevin Mazur/Getty Images for Universal Pictures/Getty Images Entertainment/Getty Images, 79; Archive Photos/Moviepix/Getty Images, 82; Kevin Winter/Getty Images for The Recording Academy/Getty Images, 85; Matt Winkelmeyer/Getty Images for dcp/Getty Images, 86; Raj Valley/Alamy, 89; Alexey Fedorenko/Shutterstock Images, 91; David Eulitt/Getty Images, 96; Mike Kemp/In Pictures/Getty Images, 99

Editor: Kari Cornell
Series Designer: Karli Hughes

Library of Congress Control Number: 2025939320

PUBLISHER'S CATALOGING-IN-PUBLICATION DATA

Names: Sonneborn, Liz, author.
Title: Taylor Swift / by Liz Sonneborn
Description: Minneapolis, Minnesota: Abdo Publishing, 2026 | Series: Modern stars | Includes online resources and index.
Identifiers: ISBN 9781098298111 (lib. bdg.) | ISBN 9798384931911 (ebook)
Subjects: LCSH: Swift, Taylor, 1989- --Juvenile literature. | Singers--United States--Biography--Juvenile literature. | Women musicians--United States--Biography--Juvenile literature. | Actors and actresses--Biography--Juvenile literature. | Businesspeople--Biography--Juvenile literature.
Classification: DDC 782.42164--dc23

CONTENTS

CHAPTER ONE

EVERYTHING FOR THE FANS

On the morning of Wednesday, October 11, 2023, it became clear that something big was about to happen at the Grove. This is a swanky outdoor shopping mall in Los Angeles, California. The Grove's social media accounts announced that all its stores and restaurants would be closed for the day.

The police began blockading streets near the mall, while news helicopters hovered overhead. Reporters noted that its cobblestone walkways were being covered with a massive red carpet. Passersby could see that the large fountain in the center of the complex was spouting water colored bright pink.

Swift arrived early to the debut of her concert film, *Taylor Swift: The Eras Tour*. She posed for photos and said hello to fans. >>

The first people to learn what was going on at the Grove were 2,200 lucky Swifties—fans of the pop music superstar Taylor Swift.[1] Swift's team had carefully selected these fans to attend the world premiere of *Taylor Swift: The Eras Tour*, a concert movie made of footage from three shows Swift had performed in nearby Inglewood, California, several months earlier.

Swift wanted to thank these fans for using their social media accounts to promote the Eras Tour. During the tour, she played 149 shows for ten million concertgoers. The events generated $2 billion in ticket sales.[2]

DRAWING A CROWD

Swift's team had a good reason to be tight-lipped about the location of the *Eras Tour* movie premiere until the last minute. A few weeks earlier Jack Antonoff, Swift's frequent collaborator, was getting married to actress Margaret Qualley on Long Beach Island in New Jersey. Many celebrities attended a dinner party for wedding guests, but only when rumors spread that Swift was there did thousands of people from across the island descend on the restaurant. Holding their cell phones high in the air to get a photo of Swift, they shouted that they wanted to see Taylor throughout the event.

Night after night, Swift performed songs from throughout her storied career. The invitees were told to come to the Grove that evening to watch the movie. It would be shown on all 14 screens in the mall's AMC theater.

THE ERAS TOUR EXPERIENCE

It was Swift's idea to make the *Eras Tour* movie for the many Swifties who were not able to attend the live concerts. Some could not afford a ticket. Others couldn't buy tickets because their nearest venue was sold out. She also knew that fans who had attended one of her concerts would love the chance to relive the fun.

The audience for the Eras Tour had developed its own fan culture. This included dressing up in outfits inspired by different eras in Swift's career. Exchanging friendship bracelets was popular as well. They often included lettered beads that spelled out song titles or lyrics.

When Swift announced the concert film on social media, she told her fans to expect a similar experience at the movie theater, including friendship bracelets, costumes from different eras, and lots of singing and dancing. The movie also promised fans who had seen the Eras Tour in person something new—a chance to see Swift in close-ups while she danced and sang their favorites of her nearly 300 recorded songs.

Swift was confident she could easily fill theater seats just by posting about the movie to her massive audience of 275 million followers on Instagram.[3] Indeed, by the time of the premiere, advance ticket sales around the

Fans sported friendship bracelets, Swift's lucky number 13, and clothing reflecting the singer's different music eras at the show in Sydney, Australia, on February 23, 2024.

globe amounted to about $100 million. This already made *Taylor Swift: The Eras Tour* one of the most successful concert movies of all time.[4]

As rumors spread about the movie premiere, hordes of Swifties made their way to the Grove. No one knew whether Swift herself was coming, but many fans gathered in the hope of catching a glimpse of the singer. Lined up along the red carpet and nearby sidewalks, they sang along as Swift's songs were played over the mall's speakers. And together they yelled and screamed when Swift posted to let her fans know she was getting in the car to go to the premiere.

Swift arrived at about six o'clock. She was decked out in an elegant strapless blue gown designed by Oscar de la Renta. The singer also wore a diamond necklace and styled her hair in a curly faux bob.

Many celebrities came to the screening, including Beyoncé, Rachel Zegler, Simu Liu, Adam Sandler, and Mariska Hargitay. But Swift spent most of her time at the theater before the premiere with her fans, not her high-profile friends. She mingled with the crowd on the edges of the red carpet, taking selfies and exchanging friendship bracelets.

PRODUCED BY TAYLOR SWIFT

When Swift decided to make an Eras Tour movie, she met with all the major film studios and streaming platforms, but in the end she chose to produce the movie herself. As a producer, she had total control over the project and was able to keep more of the profits. She negotiated directly with AMC, the largest movie theater chain in the United States, to release the film and relied on her own social media following instead of a large studio marketing budget to promote the movie.

13 OUT OF 10

Inside, the invited fans attended a reception featuring popcorn, candy, and champagne before heading to their assigned theaters. There, they anxiously waited for the movie to begin, many becoming antsy after the seven o'clock start time came and went. But in each theater, fans cheered when they realized the reason for the delay. One by one, Swift visited all 14 screenings to introduce the movie in person.

At each theater, she explained, "I've never had a fraction of the amount of fun I had on the Eras Tour before—ever."[5] She also acknowledged the hard work of her concert crew, dancers, band, and background vocalists. But she expressed her greatest gratitude to her fans. She said, "I think that you'll see that you're absolutely a main character in the film, because it was your magic and your attention to detail and your sense of humor and the ways that you lean into what I'm doing and the music I create."[6]

In the final theater, Swift added, "You're stuck with me, because I'm going to sit with you and watch this thing," prompting the audience to scream with delight.[7] Throughout the three-hour movie, like her fans, Swift sang and danced to her music.

LUCKY 13

The ticket price for the *Eras Tour* movie for kids was $13.13, and just about every Swiftie could guess why. The price doubled up her lucky number, 13. She once told MTV why she chose 13 as her lucky number during her teens. She was born on December 13, she turned 13 on Friday the thirteenth, and her first album went gold in 13 weeks. Early in her career, Swift would paint the number 13 on her hand backstage before a concert for good luck.

Swift has a strong connection to her fans, many of whom relate to the singer because of how open she is in her lyrics and on social media.

Sometimes, she pointed at the screen when she noticed something interesting and laughed at moments when she looked awkward on screen. At the end, as her song "Karma" blared, she joined her fans in standing up for an all-out dance party in the aisles.

After the show, a reporter from *Los Angeles* magazine asked audience members what they thought of the movie. One said it was "amazing." Another called it "spectacular." Still another declared the film the "best thing I've ever seen." One fan rated it "13 out of 10," and immediately burst into tears, overcome with emotion by the joyous experience she had just shared with not only her fellow Swifties but also the great Taylor Swift herself.[8]

Swift entertained the Eras Tour audiences with high-energy performances, glittery costumes, and plenty of set changes.

SWIFT'S MANY TALENTS

Swift is one of the most influential artists in contemporary music. She is also among the most famous people in the world. Some of the reasons for her enormous fame and cultural significance can be seen in the story of the *Eras Tour* concert film and its premiere.

For instance, the many aspects of Swift as a person and an artist that came through in the *Eras Tour* film help account for her success and staying power. Many musicians start losing their following after two or three albums, but Swift's ability to reinvent herself has helped her grow her audience over a nearly two-decade career. She has been able to master different genres—from country to pop to folk—while still managing to sound like herself, thereby allowing her to reach new fans without disappointing her older ones.

Swift has also shrewdly used the power of celebrity. Her mastery of social media has helped her create a zealously devoted fan base. Swift constantly provides these fans with new narratives about her life and emotions, often indirectly through clues in her lyrics, costuming, and liner notes. In this way, Swift has created a stronger relationship with her fan base than nearly any other musician has.

But the key to Swift's connection with her fans is her music. Her catchy melodies are often infectious, but her heartfelt lyrics are core to her appeal to Swifties, especially the women and girls who love her. While society often looks down on feminine emotions as silly or worthless, Swift celebrates the pain, confusion, and joy young women feel but are often ashamed to express. The passionate desire to give voice to those emotions is what made Swift determined to become a singer-songwriter from her earliest days.

CHAPTER TWO

DREAMING OF A MUSIC CAREER

Taylor Alison Swift was born in West Reading, Pennsylvania, on December 13, 1989. Her parents both had well-paying careers. Scott Swift worked for a major financial firm, while Andrea Swift was a marketing executive before she left her job to care for Taylor and Taylor's younger brother, Austin, full time.

The Swifts moved to a farm in the rural town of Wyomissing, Pennsylvania, when Taylor and Austin were young. As a side business, the family grew Christmas trees on their land. Taylor said a Christmas tree farm was "a weird place to grow up," but remembered fondly how excited she became as the

The Swift family lived at >> 78 Grandview Boulevard in Wyomissing, Pennsylvania, from when Taylor was eight until she was 14 years old.

weather turned each fall, signaling the beginning of their busy Christmas season.[1]

DISCOVERING COUNTRY MUSIC

From an early age, Taylor was interested in performing at a local theater academy. She was drawn to musical theater and won lead roles in classic musicals, such as *The Sound of Music* and *Grease*.

Also fueling Taylor's interest in singing was her discovery of country music on her sixth birthday. Her parents gave her a copy of *Blue*, the debut album of country star LeAnn Rimes. Taylor then began seeking out the work of other popular female country singers of the 1990s, such as Faith Hill, Shania Twain, and the Dixie Chicks, a group now known as The Chicks.

From there, she discovered the careers of an earlier generation of female artists. These included Patsy

GRANDMOTHER MARJORIE

In 2020, Taylor recorded the song "Marjorie," a touching tribute to her maternal grandmother, who was an opera singer. Marjorie's husband was an engineer who traveled the world to oversee the construction of bridges. Wherever they went, Marjorie always joined the local opera company. In Puerto Rico, she was the cohost of a popular radio program, *The Pan America Show*. The audience liked to poke fun at Marjorie's awkward attempts to speak Spanish, but they loved to listen to her sing.

Cline, Loretta Lynn, and Tammy Wynette, whose music often explored the lives of rural women. As she recalled, "I think it was the storytelling that really grabbed me."[2]

Her love of country music made Taylor desperately want to pursue a career in performing. Her parents saw her drive and supported her ambitions. Her mother began accompanying Taylor to New York City, where she took voice and acting lessons and auditioned for Broadway shows.

Taylor also started performing in new places. She appeared at county fairs, talent shows, wedding receptions, Boy Scout meetings, and anywhere else she could draw a crowd. At age 11, she began to sing the national anthem at sporting events.

In 2002, she sang the anthem at a Philadelphia 76ers playoff game. Sitting courtside was rapper Jay-Z, who gave her a high-five after her performance.

LeAnn Rimes was 13 years old when her song "Blue" became a smash hit in July 1996.

GOING TO NASHVILLE

Determined to become a country star, Taylor knew that to make her dream come true she would have to go to Nashville, Tennessee, the center of the country music industry. When she was 11, she persuaded her mother to take her to the city during her school's spring break. Her mother drove her up and down Music Row, the area in Nashville where all the major country music studios are located. Swift went into each record company and handed the receptionist a demo recording with her singing karaoke versions of famous country songs.

On each of the demos, Taylor had written "Call me!" but no one did. Disappointed, she decided to work even harder. She took guitar lessons from local musician Ronnie Cremer. She spent hours after school practicing and writing new melodies and lyrics. Swift knew that her devotion to songwriting made her seem weird to her peers, but she

On April 5, 2002, 12-year-old Taylor sang the national anthem before the Philadelphia 76ers played the Detroit Pistons at First Union Center.

could not stop. As she wrote in her journal, "I just have to keep writing songs. I just have to keep doing this and someday, maybe, this will be different for me."[3]

When Taylor was in the seventh grade, she noticed that her relationships with her closest friends had changed. Taylor later explained, "All of a sudden, they were cool and I wasn't anymore."[4] One day she called her friends, asking if they wanted to meet at the local mall. They all said no, each giving a different excuse. Finally, Taylor went to the mall with her mother, where they saw all those friends hanging out together in a store.

Taylor was angry, sad, and embarrassed. She processed these emotions by writing a song about the experience. It was one of the first times that Taylor realized she could use songwriting as a constructive way of expressing her feelings.

BEHIND THE MUSIC

At around ten years old, Taylor became obsessed with the television show *Behind the Music*, which aired on the cable channel VH1. Each installment documented the rise of a musical act, often followed by an account of their later fall, usually due to conflicts within a group or problems with drugs and alcohol. The show taught her an important life lesson about fame and success. These artists' downfalls came when they lost the ability to see themselves and their situations realistically. "I never wanted to make that mistake in my life, regardless of what my career ended up being," she later explained.[5]

Taylor played at the Bluebird Cafe on November 4, 2004. The singer still loves to drive by the café when she's in town.

BREAKING IN

When Taylor was 13, her parents uprooted the family and moved to Hendersonville, Tennessee, a town just outside of Nashville. Taylor wanted to get away from her old friends in Wyomissing, but she was even more desperate to start her country music career. At first, she struggled with how to break into the industry. She recalled, "I knew where I wanted to be, but I just didn't know how to get there."[6]

It was her songwriting skills that helped Taylor secure her first contract. Her parents played a part as well by connecting her with Daniel Dymtrow, a former manager of pop superstar Britney Spears. Dymtrow helped Taylor sign a development deal with RCA Records, in which the company promised to develop her as a recording artist. At 14 years old, Taylor had become the youngest songwriter to sign with the record label. After a year, RCA wanted to continue her contract, but Taylor opted out, feeling the company was moving too slowly in advancing her career.

Taylor's big break came in 2004. In that year she appeared at a talent showcase at the Bluebird Cafe. This is a legendary Nashville music venue where several country music stars were first discovered.

Her set attracted the attention of music executive Scott Borchetta, who had just started a record label called Big Machine Records. The label did not yet have an office or a staff when Borchetta told Taylor he wanted to sign her to a recording contract. "But he had a dream," she later explained. "I went with my gut instinct, which just said, 'Say yes.'"[7]

THE NAME TAYLOR

Taylor Swift's parents named her after James Taylor, one of Andrea Swift's favorite singers. With songs such as "Fire and Rain" and "Carolina in My Mind," James Taylor was one of the most beloved singer-songwriters of the 1970s. Her mother also liked that the name Taylor could be a man's or a woman's name. As a former corporate executive, Andrea Swift knew that businesses were often prejudiced against women. She thought giving her daughter a name that was neither masculine nor feminine could help her get a start in the business world one day.

CHAPTER THREE

A STAR IS BORN

At 16, Taylor at last had the record contract she had long dreamed of. But she now faced the challenge of negotiating her way through the country music industry. By the mid-2000s, country music was favoring male artists, and country radio was dominated by just a few companies. This made it harder than ever for new acts to break through.

Taylor also had to fight to write her own songs. Most country performers relied on professional songwriters. But Taylor knew that one of her greatest strengths was her songwriting. By 2005, she had already written about 150 songs. Whenever her label sent her to meet with potential songwriting collaborators, she always came armed with a stack of new songs to prove that she was already well-versed in her craft.

Taylor performed wherever she could, including at the Thanksgiving Day game between the Detroit Lions and the Miami Dolphins in 2006. >>

Taylor

Nathan Chapman and Taylor Swift worked together from 2004 through 2014.

Other songwriters, particularly older men, told her that her target audience was 35-year-old housewives and questioned whether she could write songs those fans would like. Taylor later explained, "I kept thinking, 'But I love country music, and I'm a teenager!' There have to be more kids out there like me."[1]

HER FIRST HIT

As work began on her first album, Taylor convinced her label to let her write or cowrite every song on it. She also persuaded the company to hire the relatively inexperienced Nathan Chapman to be her producer. Record producers oversee every aspect of making a recording, including choosing songs, working with sound engineers, and directing a singer's performance.

Taylor had worked with Chapman in 2004 to make several demos. He treated her with respect. Chapman was eager to hear her ideas about how her records should sound.

In anticipation of the October 2006 release of her debut album, *Taylor Swift*, Big Machine put out her first single, "Tim McGraw," in June. The idea for the song had come to Taylor her freshman year while she was in math class at Hendersonville High. She was dating a boy who was preparing to leave for college. Knowing they would soon break up, Taylor thought about all the things that would later remind him of her, including the songs of Tim McGraw, one of her favorite country artists.

Taylor had already written parts of the song before working with professional songwriter Liz Rose to refine it. Taylor later said that her brief meeting with Rose "may be the best fifteen minutes I've ever experienced."[2] The song made a slow rise on *Billboard* magazine's Hot Country Songs chart, peaking at No. 6 in January 2007. It spent eight months on the *Billboard* country singles chart.

MEETING TIM MCGRAW

In 2007, Taylor made the most of her first performance at a major televised award show. At the Country Music Awards, she sang her hit single "Tim McGraw." Midway through, she walked toward the audience, stopping at the front row before McGraw himself, who was sitting next to his superstar wife, Faith Hill. After serenading McGraw, Swift shook his hand and said, "Hi, I'm Taylor," and then hugged McGraw and Hill.[3] The audience cheered as they witnessed Swift meeting two of her idols for the first time.

PROMOTING *TAYLOR SWIFT*

The reception of "Tim McGraw" suggested that *Taylor Swift* would sell well. But Taylor didn't want to take any chances. She worked hard to promote the album. Taylor toured constantly as the opening act for stars such as Faith Hill, Rascal Flatts, George Strait, Brad Paisley, and McGraw himself.

Taylor also met with radio station executives across the country. She wanted to ensure her songs made it on the stations' playlists. She then sent handwritten thank-you notes.

The country music business has a long tradition of showing appreciation for its fans, which Taylor embraced. After shows, she would spend as much time as she could signing autographs and posing for photographs with fans. But unlike most country artists of the time, she also used the internet to connect with her audience. After signing

Taylor met Tim McGraw for the first time onstage after performing her hit song at the annual Academy of Country Music Awards event in May 2007.

her first contract at 14, Taylor set up a page on Myspace, a social media platform where she posted new music, personal photos, and answers to questions from fans.

By the time she was promoting *Taylor Swift*, she had nearly 700,000 followers on the platform.[4] Many of those followers were teenage girls. They related to the wholesome, girl-next-door image Taylor cultivated.

Taylor also left messages for fans in the printed lyrics booklet included with the *Taylor Swift* CD. She used capital letters to spell out words and phrases. For example, her secret message in the lyrics to the breakup song "Picture to Burn" read "DATE NICE BOYS." This encouraged fans to buy a physical copy of her album, thereby maximizing the revenue from *Taylor Swift*.

Taylor's promotional efforts paid off. *Taylor Swift* spent a full 24 weeks at the No. 1 spot on the Top Country Albums chart. The album produced five singles, including "Our Song," a buoyant tune celebrating young love that Taylor wrote as a freshman for a high school talent contest. It spent six weeks at the top of the *Billboard* country singles chart, making Taylor the youngest person in chart history to write and perform a number one country song.

With the success of *Taylor Swift*, Taylor also won accolades from her peers. In 2007, she won the Horizon Award from the Country Music Association (CMA), which recognizes rising musicians. She was nominated by the Academy of Country Music (ACM) for Top New Female Vocalist and earned a Grammy nomination for Best New Artist, but she did not win these awards.

This was also the year Taylor graduated from high school. After her sophomore year at Hendersonville High she had transferred to Aaron Academy, which allowed her to finish her schooling at home. This was a better fit with her busy touring schedule.

"I can't even believe this is real. This is definitely the highlight of my senior year."[5]

—Taylor Swift accepting the Horizon Award for best new artist at the 2007 Country Music Association Awards

BEING FEARLESS

Swift attended her first MTV Video Music Awards (VMAs) in September 2008 as a nominee for the Best New Artist award, which went to Tokio Hotel. Swift arrived at the event with her new boyfriend, singer Joe Jonas of the Jonas Brothers. Swift and Jonas had quietly started dating the previous summer, and Swift had appeared onstage at several Jonas Brothers concerts.

But Swift was far less quiet about their breakup, which happened just a few weeks after the VMAs. In November, while promoting her new album *Fearless* on *The Ellen DeGeneres Show*, she revealed that Jonas had broken up with her during a 25-second phone conversation. The story made headlines, and Swift became even more relatable to young female fans, many of whom had their own tales of romances gone wrong.

Swift attended the VMAs with Joe Jonas in September 2008.

The story also proved to be an excellent promotion for *Fearless*, which sold more than half a million copies in its first week. In the months before the album came out, the song "Love Story" was released and advertised to both country and pop music fans. The song was a country hit, but it also became Swift's first single to cross over to the pop charts. It spent 49 weeks on the *Billboard* Hot 100, where it peaked at No. 4.

Swift's other runaway hit from *Fearless* was "You Belong With Me." The song was about an uncool high school girl pining away for a boy who was dating the head cheerleader. Swift explained that the lyrics came from her own experience with "girl-next-door-itis, where the guy is friends with you and that's it."[6]

The song's music video played out like a teen movie. It ended with Swift as the lovesick narrator finally winning

THE CHRISTMAS EP

Well-known for loving Christmas, Swift gave her fans a special gift in late 2007 when she released *Sounds of the Season: The Taylor Swift Holiday Collection*. The EP featured four country-flavored covers of the popular Christmas songs "Silent Night," "White Christmas," "Santa Baby," and "Last Christmas." Swift insisted on adding two original songs—"Christmas Must Be Something More" and "Christmases When You Were Mine."

the boy of her dreams at a school dance. "You Belong With Me" became her biggest hit at this point in her career, topping the Hot Country Songs chart and hitting No. 2 on the *Billboard* Hot 100.

The success of *Fearless* led to Swift's first tour as a headliner. It began in April 2009 and lasted more than 15 months, with dates in the United States, Canada, England, and Australia. Tickets quickly sold out.

Swift knew just what kind of show she wanted. She oversaw the costumes, which included a marching band outfit, a wedding dress, and several sparkling dresses. She also worked with set designers to realize her vision for the stage. The most elaborate set was a brightly lit fairy-tale castle. The Fearless Tour grossed $66.5 million and was attended by 1.2 million fans.[7] With a sensational tour, a debut album that sold more than three million copies, and a string of hits, Swift had proven herself to be a star.[8]

"FIFTEEN"

On February 8, 2009, Swift performed at the Grammy Awards for the first time, singing a duet with Miley Cyrus of the *Fearless* song "Fifteen." The song is a tribute to Swift's close friend, Abigail Anderson, whom Swift met on her first day at Hendersonville High School. Over the years, Swift and Anderson have remained friends. Anderson attended the 2015 Grammys as Swift's date, and Swift served as a bridesmaid at Anderson's 2017 wedding.

CHAPTER FOUR

TAKING CONTROL

On September 13, 2009, Swift sat in the audience for the MTV VMAs. She was due to perform later in the night, but first she waited for the announcement of the Best Female Video. This was the only category in which she had been nominated.

Her video for "You Belong With Me" had been widely celebrated, but she was not expected to win. A country artist had never won a VMA, and her competition was extremely stiff, with the other nominees including Kelly Clarkson, Katy Perry, Pink, and Lady Gaga. But it was Beyoncé, nominated for her groundbreaking black-and-white dance video for

In 2009, Swift won her first VMA, and she won several more as her career progressed. >>

"Single Ladies (Put a Ring on It)," who seemed most likely to take the award.

Soon after the show began, actor Taylor Lautner, then Swift's boyfriend, came onstage to announce the Best Female Video winner. When he opened the envelope and shouted, "Taylor Swift!" the camera turned to Swift, who looked thrilled and genuinely surprised. She took the stage wearing a shimmering silver gown and told the crowd, "I always dreamed about what it would be like to maybe win one of these someday."[1]

Suddenly, rapper Kanye West jumped onstage, grabbed the microphone from Swift's hand, and said, "Yo Taylor, I'm really happy for you and I'mma let you finish, but Beyoncé has one of the best videos of all time. One of the best videos of all time!"[2] He left the stage as Swift

VALENTINE'S DAY

In 2010, Swift made her movie debut in the romantic comedy *Valentine's Day*. With just under five minutes of screen time, Swift plays Felicia, a bubbly high school student devoted to her boyfriend Willie, played by Lautner. Swift and Lautner briefly dated after meeting on the set. Although the movie was poorly reviewed, it was a hit at the box office. Swift fans got to enjoy a goofy dance by Swift's character, a reference to her lucky number 13, and her songs "Today Was a Fairytale" and "Jump Then Fall," which appeared on the movie's soundtrack.

After she accepted her award for Video of the Year, Beyoncé invited Swift to finish her speech.

stood silently, looking devastated because as the crowd booed West's rudeness, she thought they were booing her and suggesting she did not deserve the award.

Swift left the stage without saying another word and began to cry, but she quickly pulled herself together because she had to perform. Five minutes later, Swift enthusiastically sang "You Belong With Me" to an audience of millions on live television as though nothing unusual had happened. She later explained, "I just told myself I had to perform, and I tried to convince myself that maybe this wasn't that big of a deal."[3] At the end of the night, Beyoncé won Video of the Year.

FACING BACKLASH

Despite Swift's hopes, the West incident turned out to be an extremely big deal, with his actions widely condemned by entertainment reporters and celebrities. Even President Barack Obama sharply criticized West. The discussions brought Swift into the spotlight but not in a way she appreciated. Instead of being acknowledged as a talented singer-songwriter at the top of her game, she was portrayed in the press as a victim of male aggression, too young and delicate to defend herself.

But Swift soon had proof of her talents. At the 52nd Grammy Awards, held on January 31, 2010, *Fearless* won the Grammy for Album of the Year, making 20-year-old Swift the youngest winner of that award yet. Swift, who was nominated for a total of eight Grammys, including Song of the Year and Record of the Year for "You Belong With Me," won three other Grammys. These were Best Country Album, Best Country Song for "White Horse," and Best Female Country Vocal Performance for "White Horse."

Swift's Grammy triumph, however, was tarnished by the reception of her duet on the show. She performed "You Belong With Me" and the Fleetwood Mac song "Rhiannon" with rock legend Stevie Nicks. Critics took Swift to task for singing slightly off-key.

Swift performed with Stevie Nicks at the 52nd Grammy Awards in January 2010.

Particularly scathing was a post by music journalist Bob Lefsetz who wrote, “Now everybody knows that Taylor Swift can’t sing. . . . Taylor’s too young and dumb to understand the mistake she made."[4] His words made Swift angry enough to write a response with the song "Mean."

In addition to claims that she was a bad singer, Swift also had to weather general backlash following her Album of the Year win. Some journalists questioned whether she actually wrote her own songs. Others speculated that her success was engineered by older male collaborators who manipulated her behind the scenes.

THE TERM *SWIFTIE*

"My fans came up with a name for themselves, and it's so cute," Swift exclaimed in a 2012 promotional video.[5] The video was possibly Swift's first public acknowledgment of the term *Swiftie*. It was in common use by early 2010. Swift registered a trademark for Swifties in 2017. In 2023, *Swiftie* was a finalist for Oxford Dictionary's Word of the Year, losing out to the slang term *rizz*, a shortened form of the word *charisma*.

SPEAK NOW

Swift took all these attacks to heart. She began taking voice lessons again, determined that no one would ever be able to legitimately criticize her singing again. She also decided that on her next album, *Speak Now*, she would be the sole writer on every song. Swift chose the album's title because of her strengthened resolve to speak her mind through her music.

Although many of her previous songs had been autobiographical, for *Speak Now*, Swift leaned more heavily into stories about her personal experiences, particularly those relating to her romantic life. In interviews, she declined to say that particular songs were about certain romantic partners. But fans were usually able to figure out references to her famous boyfriends.

One of her more obvious clues was the title of the ballad "Dear John." It was commonly seen as a dissection of her relationship with singer John Mayer. The scathing lyrics take him to task for playing mind games with her that she was too young to handle.

"Better Than Revenge" was seen as a rock-influenced takedown of Jonas's girlfriend Camilla Belle. Some critics labeled the song as a mean-spirited misdirection of her anger toward Jonas. Swift, however, showed a new maturity in "Back to December," in which she accepted responsibility for ruining a romance by neglecting an attentive, loving boyfriend. The ballad is believed to be about her failed relationship with Lautner.

In the song "Innocent," Swift reflected on West's behavior at the 2009 VMAs. The lyrics offered forgiveness by acknowledging that what a person does is not necessarily who they are. She performed the song for

James Taylor, the singer after whom Swift was named, joined her onstage in New York during her Speak Now Tour. They performed James Taylor's song "Fire and Rain" together.

the first time at the VMAs in 2010 as a sign that she had forgiven West.

With the release of *Speak Now* on October 25, 2010, Swift became the first country artist to sell one million copies of an album in its first week. In 2011 Swift was named *Billboard's* Woman of the Year. Although the reviews for *Speak Now* did not match the critical success of her previous album, she won Grammys for Best Country Solo Performance and Best Country Song for "Mean." The Speak Now World Tour included 110 shows in North America, South America, Europe, and Asia. It was the highest grossing tour for a female artist in 2011.

RED

One day, when Swift and her band were preparing for the Speak Now Tour, Swift was in a sour mood over a fading relationship. As she often did, she began strumming her guitar and singing about what she was feeling. The other musicians chimed in, and they improvised a song.

Swift brought in Rose, her regular collaborator, to help edit the song into a version that ran 5.5 minutes. Filled with sadness, anger, and regret, the song, titled "All Too Well," became a fan favorite. It appeared on Swift's album *Red*, which was released on October 22, 2012.

Swift had originally planned to have Chapman produce *Red*. But midway through the project, she decided she wanted to try new sounds and musical genres. While many *Red* tracks, such as "All Too Well," sounded like songs on her other country albums, she included several songs that delved into the pop and rock trends of the moment.

> **"I love my life, I love my career, I love my friends—but things are not okay all the time. So I don't sing about things being okay all the time."[6]**
>
> **—Taylor Swift, 2013**

To guide her, she turned to Swedish producers Max Martin and Johan "Shellback" Schuster. Martin was a celebrated hitmaker. He had previously worked with

THE RED TOUR

With the 2013 tour promoting her *Red* album, Swift graduated from playing arenas to playing stadiums. The shows featured giant screens, confetti drops, a gymnastics routine, and nonstop screaming from thousands of fans dressed in red. The tour also skillfully combined massive production numbers with intimate moments. The emotional climax of the show started with "I Knew You Were Trouble," during which 15 elaborately costumed dancers performed a masquerade ball. Then Swift sat alone at her piano for a moving rendition of "All Too Well," as the audience sang along.

Spears, Perry, NSYNC, and the Backstreet Boys.

With Martin and Shellback, Swift created "22." The song celebrated the joys and confusion she and her friends felt at that age. They also wrote the rock hit "I Knew You Were Trouble," rumored to be about her romance with singer Harry Styles, a member of One Direction.

But their greatest collaboration was "We Are Never Ever Getting Back Together." This exuberant pop tune is about a young woman determined to end an exhausting on-again, off-again relationship. The song became her first No. 1 single on the *Billboard* Hot 100. "We Are Never Ever Getting Back Together" was also nominated for Record of the Year at the Grammys.

Big Machine Records was worried about how country fans would react to her new sound. But "We Are Never Ever Getting Back Together" went to No. 1 on the *Billboard*

Hot Country Songs chart. "I Knew You Were Trouble" was frequently played on country radio.

Record companies set music genres based on certain traits. Country music is defined as songs featuring string instruments that are inspired by folk, blues, Western, and gospel music. Instead of alienating her core audience, Swift's new sound had only added pop and rock lovers to her fan base, making her more popular than ever. The success of *Red* provided Swift with an important lesson. In popular music, constant reinvention was a proven way of staying on top.

At the *Billboard* Music Awards in 2013, Swift took home six awards, including Best Country Album, Top Country Artist, and Best Country Song for "We Are Never Ever Getting Back Together."

CHAPTER FIVE

1989

In January 2013, Swift was still riding high from the successful launch of *Red* when she attended the Golden Globe Awards as a nominee for the song "Safe & Sound" from the movie *The Hunger Games*. But when hosts Tina Fey and Amy Poehler made a joke about Swift during the ceremony, it had nothing to do with her music career. Instead, it was a jab at her highly publicized love life.

Fey said Swift should "stay away from Michael J. Fox's son"—a reference to Sam Michael Fox, a young actor who was handing out statues that night as "Mr. Golden Globe." After Poehler encouraged Swift to "go for it," Fey added, "No, she needs some me-time to learn about herself."[1]

The audience laughed at their digs, but Swift was not amused. She had grown tired of constant gossip

Taylor Swift attended the 2013 Golden Globes in a deep purple gown by Donna Karan Atelier. >>

OBE
RDS
GLO
AWA

about her in the entertainment press, which painted her as a boy-crazy, obsessed girlfriend, determined to get back at her exes by writing mean songs about them. She was particularly upset because, in the previous three years, she had dated only two men, Styles and Conor Kennedy, son of the famous politician Robert F. Kennedy Jr.

Swift was further annoyed by the way the press covered romances of male celebrities. Swift claimed they were celebrated as living life to the fullest, while she was shamed and judged. Angry at what she regarded as yet another sexist comment at her expense, Swift lashed out at Fey and Poehler in an interview with *Vanity Fair* magazine. Recalling an old quotation attributed to the political figure Madeleine Albright, she said,

EXPERIENCING SEXISM

Many female recording artists say that sexism in the music industry leaves them feeling diminished and disrespected. Early in her career, Swift did not notice any sexist treatment. As she told *Vogue* in 2019, "Men in the industry saw me as a kid . . . who reminded them more of their little niece or daughter than a successful woman in business." Only as Swift grew older and became more successful did she notice hostility from male colleagues. She said, "As soon as I started playing stadiums—when I started to look like a woman—that wasn't as cool anymore."[2]

"There's a special place in hell for women who don't help other women."[3]

CHANGING HER IMAGE

Exhausted by similar commentary about her online, Swift retreated from the social media accounts that she had earlier used so well to cultivate her celebrity. For months she posted so infrequently on Instagram that she forgot her password. Swift not only tried to ignore the old public narrative about her but also actively worked to create a new one.

Central to that effort was shying away from romantic relationships in favor of public friendships with a variety of young women who, like her, were making their way in glamorous industries, such as fashion and entertainment. Members of what Swift called her "squad" included comedian Lena Dunham, actress Selena Gomez, singer Lorde, and Alana, Danielle, and Este Haim of the rock band Haim. Perhaps her closest friend at the time was model Karlie Kloss, who Swift met at the Victoria's Secret Fashion Show in 2013.

As part of her new image, Swift had her hair cut and straightened and publicly embraced feminism for the first time. Eager to live away from her family, she

In 2013, Swift stepped back from romantic relationships and focused on spending more time with friends, such as Selena Gomez.

bought an apartment in New York City in 2014. This was something Swift thought she'd never do, as she didn't know if she'd like living in such a big, busy city. But after relocating there, she embraced the city's vibrancy and became one of New York's most high-profile boosters.

The move from Nashville to New York was also symbolic of a shift in her musical taste. Swift was being drawn more toward pop and dance music than the country genre. Some critics had complained that *Red*, by mixing country and pop songs, did not have a cohesive sound.

Swift realized that, although she liked both styles of music, the time had come to pick one. As she worked on the album that would become *1989*, named after the year of her birth, Swift turned away from her Nashville collaborators. She more fully embraced Martin and Shellback.

They helped her craft a sound that drew from the electronic dance music that was then topping the charts. Swift was insistent that the songwriting had to be solid. She was leery of adding a dance break, beat change, or other new musical element that had "nothing to do with the feeling . . . nothing to do with the emotion . . . nothing to do with the lyric."[4]

TIES TO NASHVILLE

Although Swift largely left behind country music with her album *1989*, she has retained close ties to her adopted city of Nashville. In October 2013, the city's Country Music Hall of Fame and Museum opened the Taylor Swift Education Center, which she funded with a $4 million donation.[5] The center offers music and art workshops for school groups and families interested in learning about the history and culture of country music.

TAKING A RISK

The executives at Big Machine Records were unhappy with her new direction. They took her aside and told her that she was making a big mistake. They told her she was abandoning her devoted country music following.

They urged her to add fiddle or steel-guitar solos to give the songs a more country feel. But Swift was adamant that the only way to keep her act fresh was to try a new sound. She felt she needed to take big risks to stay relevant.

As the release date for *1989* neared, Swift started reconnecting with her most devoted fans to figure out whether they would accept her new direction. She returned to reading comments and posting on social media. Swift's team also began organizing events called Secret Sessions in her various homes. For each session, the team would invite 89 superfans they found on Instagram, Tumblr, and Twitter (now X). For four hours, Swift would

In the role of Rosemary in *The Giver*, Swift wore a brown wig, as director Phillip Noyce wanted to make her less recognizable.

play her latest tracks, tell her guests stories about the songs, and ask for their opinion of the music and lyrics.

On August 15, 2014, *The Giver*, a film adaptation of Lois Lowry's classic 1993 young adult novel, was released. Swift briefly appeared in the part of Rosemary, the emotionless daughter of the title character, who is the only person in the novel's dystopian world able to remember the past. A modest box office success, it mostly drew negative reviews from critics.

Swift's performance about a week later at the VMAs was received with much more enthusiasm.

Swift premiered "Shake It Off," the lead single from *1989*, ahead of the album's planned release in October. In the energetic performance, she and a crew of dancers shimmied across an elaborate set featuring huge numbers spelling out the name of the album.

Midway through the performance, Swift stood atop the giant "1989" prop, seemingly preparing to jump down to be caught by the dancers below. But she changed her mind, telling the audience she was not going to jump. The song stopped as she climbed down and ended the performance on the set below.

A NEW ATTITUDE

The lively, self-consciously funny performance was a perfect introduction to her new album, showcasing not only her new sound but also her new attitude. The lyrics of "Shake It Off" directly addressed the "haters" who leveled criticism and insults at her. The cheerful dance song announced her determination to do what she wanted without worrying about what

> **"I've never ever felt edgy, cool, or sexy. Not one time. And it's not important for [my young fans] to be those things. It's important for them to be imaginative, intelligent, hardworking, strong, smart, quick-witted, charming."** [6]
>
> **—Taylor Swift, 2014**

anyone else thought. A global hit, "Shake It Off" debuted at No. 1 on the *Billboard* Hot 100.

Her sense of humor was also on full display in "Blank Space." According to Swift, the song took the perspective of "a girl who's crazy but seductive but glamorous but nuts but manipulative"—in essence, the type of woman the press had long falsely accused her of being.[7] The song became her third No. 1 single on the *Billboard* Hot 100.

As she had done many times before, she used the lyrics of the catchy "Bad Blood" to call out the bad behavior of a nemesis. This song was not an attack on an old boyfriend but on a former female friend who had crossed her. Fans and the press figured out that she was was referring to singer Katy Perry, whom Swift accused of trying to sabotage her by hiring some of Swift's tour dancers behind her back. The star-studded video featured many of Swift's female friends, including Karlie Kloss, Selena Gomez, and Lena Dunham.

There were some love songs on *1989*, most notably "Clean" and "Out of the Woods." Both are allegedly about Harry Styles. A collaboration with British indie artist Imogen Heap, "Clean" describes getting over a lost love well enough to be able to wish an ex well. For "Out of the Woods," Swift worked with musician and songwriter Jack

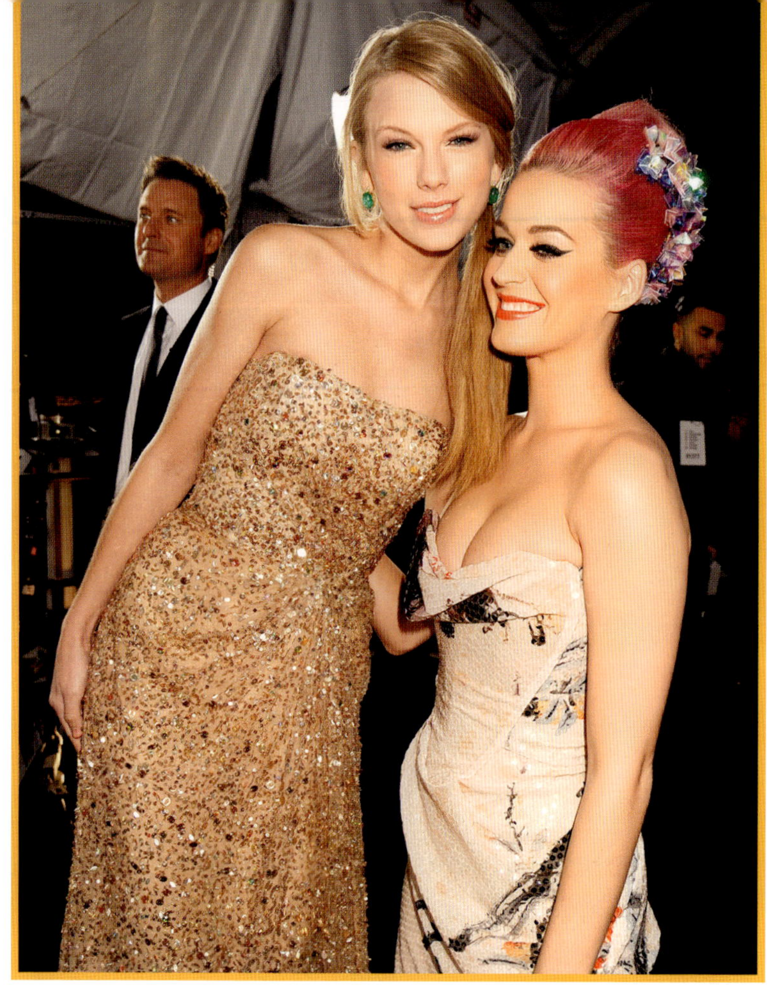

Swift and Perry became friends in 2008 and spent time together at many awards shows, including the American Music Awards in 2011.

Antonoff, whom she had worked with in 2013 to make "Sweeter than Fiction." Antonoff would become one of her most frequent collaborators. "Out of the Woods" is about the anxiety of living within a strained romantic relationship that threatened to crumble at any minute.

A RUNAWAY SUCCESS

Commercially, *1989* was a runaway success, proving the wisdom of Swift's daring move to transform herself from a country singer to an international pop star. The album sold almost 1.3 million copies in its first week.[8] Bolstered by its string of hit singles, *1989* hit No. 1 on the *Billboard* 200 album chart and managed to stay in the top 10 for a full year.

The 1989 World Tour was equally successful, grossing more than $250 million. Its 85 shows were seen by about 2.2 million fans, many of whom scoured social media to discover everything about playlists, sets, and costume changes before they saw the show.[9] To restore the element of surprise, Swift recruited famous guest stars to perform with her at each stop. Her guests included Dunham, Mary J. Blige, Mick Jagger, Kobe Bryant, and Matt LeBlanc.

TAKING ON STREAMING

In 2014, Swift publicly criticized the music streaming service Spotify. Swift complained about the tiny payments the service gave to artists when their songs were streamed by customers and argued that Spotify paid artists nothing at all for songs streamed during free trial periods. A week after the release of *1989*, she removed her entire catalog from Spotify, Pandora, and other streaming sites, an act of defiance seen as a strike for artists' rights. Swift continued to sell her music through Apple, which agreed to pay royalties during free periods. When Spotify raised its royalties in 2017, Swift made her songs again accessible to Spotify users.

Swift performed at New York City's Times Square during the *Good Morning America* show in October 2014.

For Swift, one of the most exciting guests was Natalie Maines, lead singer of The Chicks. Maines and the other members of her group had been blacklisted by the music industry for speaking out against President George W. Bush in 2003. Then the group was re-embraced by their fans during a world tour three years later.

Standing beside Maines, Swift spoke to the crowd. "If not for this woman and her band, I would not have known that you could be quirky and fun and yourself and outspoken and brave and real," she said.[10] Feeling emboldened by her recent success, Swift could not have foreseen that she, like Maines, was about to be caught up in such a fierce backlash that she would be forced to retreat from the spotlight as well.

CHAPTER SIX

FIGHTING BACK

On February 15, 2016, Swift won the Grammy Award for Album of the Year for *1989*. She was the youngest person to win the award twice, but in her acceptance speech, she was more interested in addressing another statistic—that she was the first woman to receive two Album of the Year Grammys. Speaking directly to young women, she said, "There are going to be people along the way who will try to undercut your success or take credit for your accomplishments or your fame."[1]

Swift was not just offering generic advice but was commenting on recent events relating to her career. A few days before the Grammy ceremony, West had released his latest album, *The Life of Pablo*. One song, "Famous," contained a vulgar line about Swift: "I feel like me and Taylor might still have sex.

In February 2016, Swift's *1989* won Grammy Awards for Album of the Year, Best Pop Vocal Album, and Best Music Video for "Bad Blood." >>

Why? I made that b— famous."[2] West was referring to the incident during the 2009 VMAs when he interrupted her acceptance speech for Best Female Video.

Since that time, Swift and West had appeared to have reconciled their differences. In 2015, Swift had socialized with West and his wife, Kim Kardashian, at the Grammys. Later that year, at West's request, Swift had presented him with the Video Vanguard Award at the VMAs. She told the press, "To now be in a place where Kanye and I respect each other—that's one of my *favorite* things that has happened in my career."[3]

West claimed that he and Swift had talked on the phone before he released "Famous," and she had given him her blessing. Swift's publicist, however, said Swift objected strongly to the lyrics about her. The publicist insisted West had not told Swift the exact wording of the lyrics.

"TAYLOR IS A SNAKE"

The angry back-and-forth came amid a new popular backlash to Swift following the success of *1989*. In articles and social media posts, people complained that she was picking fights with other celebrities. They said that Swift then painted herself as the victim.

At the Grammy Awards on February 8, 2015, Swift and West talked about recording music together.

In an October 2015 interview, pop culture critic Chuck Klosterman voiced another common complaint he had heard about Swift, saying someone had called her "calculating." Swift shot back, "But here was someone taking a positive thing—the fact that I think about things and that I care about my work—and trying to make that into an insinuation about my personal life. Highly offensive."[4]

Within this climate, the romantic relationship between Swift and Calvin Harris, a record producer and DJ, ended in June 2016 after they had dated for 15 months. At first, the split seemed amicable. But on July 13,

MET GALA LOOKS

Between 2008 and 2016, Swift made six appearances at the Met Gala, an annual museum fundraiser at which celebrities wear elaborate outfits that interpret the gala's theme. Swift wore an off-the-shoulder white gown by Ralph Lauren for the 2010 theme "American Woman: Fashioning a National Identity" and a black J. Mendel dress with cutouts paired with smoky eye makeup for the 2013 theme "PUNK: Chaos and Couture."

Swift's representatives acknowledged that she had secretly helped write "This Is What You Came For," a hit single performed by Harris and the singer Rihanna.

Harris responded with a series of angry posts on Twitter. He said that, by revealing her role in writing the song, Swift had undermined his contributions to the record. Harris made a reference to Swift's old feud with singer Katy Perry before signing off. Fans of Harris responded with snake emojis on Swift's social media posts as a way of accusing her being conniving and deceitful.

Four days later, Kim Kardashian added fuel to the fire by posting a series of videos on Snapchat showing Kanye West speaking on the phone to Swift about "Famous." The videos were edited to suggest that Swift was told about all the song lyrics and that she gave her permission to release it. This was presented as evidence that she had lied about the conversation.

> “A mass public shaming, with millions of people saying you are quote-unquote *canceled*, is a very isolating experience.”[6]
>
> —Taylor Swift, 2019

In 2020, a complete recording of the call was leaked on social media. It revealed that Swift, as she had said, was not told about the lyric calling her a "b—." But in 2016, the edited video inspired West fans to respond to posts about Swift on social media with a torrent of snake emojis, as the hashtag #TaylorIsaSnake took off.

RETREATING TO LONDON

Swift responded with an Instagram post that ended, "I would very much like to be excluded from this narrative, one that I have never asked to be part of, since 2009."[5] Her words set off another round of criticism. People pointed out that through her song "Innocent" and her latest Grammy speech, she had already contributed to the narrative she said she wanted nothing to do with.

She came under further fire for her brief summer romance with actor Tom Hiddleston. Her critics claimed it was a fake relationship. They said she was dating him to distract everyone from her supposed lying.

The outpouring of hate shook Swift to her core. Years later, she reflected on that time in a documentary about

Swift and Alwyn managed to keep their relationship private for months before the first photos of the pair appeared in the press in May 2017.

her life. In the film, she told her mom, "When people decided I was wicked and evil and conniving and not a good person, that was the [criticism] that I couldn't really bounce back from."[7]

Swift responded to the criticism by withdrawing from social media. She also retreated from the public eye, spending nearly a year in London, England, where she barely ever left her rented house. She spent much of her time with her new boyfriend, British actor Joe Alwyn, whom she likely first met in May 2016 at the Met Gala.

Swift's relationship with Alwyn helped restore her mental stability during this difficult time. She also turned to her music to feel more in control of her life. She later explained that making music about the experience had been the best way for her to cope with the backlash. The songs she wrote became her sixth studio album, which she appropriately named *reputation*.

JOE ALWYN

When Swift met her soon-to-be boyfriend Joe Alwyn in 2016, he was a young British actor with few credits to his name. But months later, Swift attended the premiere of his first movie, *Billy Lynn's Long Halftime Walk*. His starring role earned him critical praise and more acting opportunities. Alwyn has since appeared in many big movies, including *The Favourite* in 2018, *The Souvenir: Part II* in 2021, and *The Brutalist* in 2024.

SPEAKING OUT

Even as Swift tried to retreat from the world, she continued to face challenges. Swift was dealing with a court case arising out of a 2013 interview with David Mueller, a prominent country DJ in Colorado. After the interview, Swift had her photo taken with Mueller. As the photographer snapped their picture, Mueller reached under Swift's skirt and grabbed her rear end, causing her to squirm, but he would not let go of her.

On August 14, 2017, Taylor Swift's brother, Austin, *left*, and publicist, Tree Paine, *center*, arrived at the Alfred A. Arraj Courthouse in Denver, Colorado, for the trial against Mueller.

Privately, Swift told his employer about the assault, and after an investigation, Mueller was fired. In September 2015, Mueller filed a lawsuit against Swift seeking millions in damages, claiming she had defamed him. She soon launched a countersuit, accusing him of sexual assault. Wanting to send a message rather than bankrupt Mueller, she asked for only symbolic damages of $1.[8]

In early August 2017, the trial began. The evidence against Mueller was substantial, including Swift's own eyewitness account. She held her own while Mueller's attorney grilled her on the stand, asking her questions about why she did not scream or react quickly to the alleged assault. The experience filled her with fury.

Swift later recalled, "I was angry I had to be there. I was angry that this happens to women. I was angry that people are paid to antagonize the victim."[9] In the end, however, the jury believed Swift and found Mueller guilty of sexual assault and battery.

After the verdict, Swift was widely praised for courageously standing up for herself. Not long before, she had feared she would never come back after being "canceled." In Swift's case, this meant no longer being supported by a group of very vocal online followers. But suddenly she was not only embraced again by the public but also portrayed as a feminist hero in the press. Swift, however, was poised to test all the hard-earned goodwill she received by releasing what would become the most provocative and controversial album of her career.

THE #METOO MOVEMENT

Two months after Swift won her sexual assault case against Mueller, the widespread #MeToo movement swept the United States. Millions of women who had been victims of sexual harassment and assault began speaking about their experiences in social media posts. *Time* magazine honored their actions by naming "Silence Breakers" as its 2017 Person of the Year. The magazine included Swift as one of the most notable Silence Breakers for making her sexual assault public even before the #MeToo movement offered support to those speaking out.

CHAPTER SEVEN

BOLDER THAN EVER

In late August 2017, a post appeared on Swift's social media accounts. The grainy video showed a slithering snake's tail. It was a prelude to her announcement that her *reputation* album would be released in November.

On August 27, Swift premiered her music video of the album's lead single, "Look What You Made Me Do" at the VMAs. The video made clear that, after her long retreat from public life, she was roaring back into the spotlight. And instead of shying away from her detractors' criticisms, she was ready to take them on.

"Look What You Made Me Do" was more vocally subdued and featured synthesizers and drum

Swift's *reputation* album and tour garnered mixed reviews from fans and critics for its dark lyrics and sound. >>

DECIPHERING THE "LOOK" VIDEO

The "Look What You Made Me Do" video had so many references to Swift's career that some fans had trouble puzzling them all out. Superfan Lauren Lipman made a YouTube video that cataloged all the clues she found. Swift saw the video and liked it so much that she included it in a montage shown on screens before each show during the Reputation Tour. Lipman's sleuthing was so successful that she was able to turn managing her YouTube channel about all things Taylor into a full-time career.

machines, making it one of Swift's darkest songs yet. The video began with Swift emerging from a grave, ready to take revenge. This angrier persona communicated with her critics through a spoken line in the song: "I'm sorry, the old Taylor can't come to the phone right now. Why? Oh, 'cause she's dead!"[1]

The images in the video were filled with inside information and jokes that Swift knew fans would love to decipher. These included references to the $1 in damages she was awarded in the Mueller case and of course the infamous #TaylorIsaSnake. The video ended with a line of Swifts dressed in costumes from various points in her career, spouting out all the criticisms that had infuriated Swift over the years.

CHAOS AND CALM

Many critics slammed the single. *Vulture* called it "the worst music of her career," and *USA Today* declared that Swift had "never been more exhausting."[2] But the video got her fans and foes talking. It set a record for the number of times a video was viewed during its first 24 hours on YouTube. The song debuted at No. 77 on the *Billboard* Hot 100 before shooting to No. 1, a position it held for three weeks.

In 2023, *Time* magazine described *reputation* as "a goth-punk moment of female rage at being gaslit by the entire social structure."[3] Certainly, many songs on the album are as dramatic as "Look What You Made Me Do." "Getaway Car" compares romantic woes to a crime spree, and "This Is Why We Can't Have Nice Things" seems to reference West and mocks the idea of forgiving someone's past wrongs.

But *reputation* also includes songs with a softer sound, such as the radio hit "Delicate," which explores nervousness and fear amidst the rush of a new crush. "New Year's Day" celebrates the support a romantic partner can provide. The mix of chaos and calm in *reputation* likely reflected Swift's growing affection for Alwyn, even while she had been in turmoil. Alwyn was hesitant to talk about his private life, but by May 2018, he and Swift were comfortable enough in their relationship to post about it on Instagram.

Swift's Reputation Tour featured a giant inflatable snake and pyrotechnics.

Swift has sometimes reflected that the *reputation* era was the lowest point of her career, but it was the best-selling album of 2017. Swift's tour for *reputation* was also an enormous success, best remembered for the giant inflatable snake that dominated its set design. In 2019, Swift said, "I can't tell you how hard I had to keep from laughing every time my 63-foot [19 m] inflatable cobra named Karyn appeared onstage in front of 60,000 screaming fans."[4] Indeed, she had emerged from her lowest point to stage an amazing comeback.

NO MORE NICE GIRL

As Swift's music became bolder, so did her ideas about herself as a public figure. Throughout her career, she had been warned never to discuss politics. Record executives constantly held out the example of The Chicks, a band that had nearly been drummed out of country music for a political comment, as a cautionary tale.

Swift had also been conditioned under all circumstances to be what she called "a nice girl." As she explained, "A nice girl doesn't force their opinion on people. A nice girl smiles and waves and says thank you. A nice girl doesn't make people feel uncomfortable with her views."[5]

But in 2018, things changed. Swift felt she could no longer keep her political views to herself. In that year's midterm elections in Tennessee, Republican Marsha Blackburn was running against former Democratic governor Phil Bredesen for an open seat in the US Senate.

Swift strongly opposed Blackburn, who voted against reauthorizing the Violence Against Women Act. This law provided protections for women against domestic

TRACK FIVE

"Delicate," the fifth song on *reputation*, is what fans call a typical track five—an emotionally powerful song that Swift tends to slot into that spot on each album. At first the positioning of such songs was not a conscious decision but something that came about naturally. Swift later explained, "As I was making albums I guess I was just kind of putting a very vulnerable, personal, honest, emotional song as track five."[6] Other notable track fives include "All Too Well" on *Red*, "White Horse" on *Fearless*, and "Dear John" on *Speak Now*.

violence, sexual assault, and stalking. Blackburn also did not support same-sex marriage and LGBTQ+ rights, whereas Swift did. Swift publicly endorsed Bredesen and encouraged young people to register to vote. Despite Swift's efforts, Blackburn won the election.

Swift was also growing braver in her business dealings. With *reputation*, she had satisfied her commitment to deliver six albums to Big Machine Records, as specified in her original contract with the company. Her dealings with Borchetta at Big Machine had long been strained, as he fought her decision to move from country to pop and rock music.

She was also upset that Borchetta would not negotiate a fair deal for her to gain the rights to the master recordings of her albums with Big Machine. Big Machine held the rights to the masters. This meant the company had complete control over licensing arrangements for those recordings.

Swift met with Lucian Grainge, the executive in charge of Universal Music Group, and Monte Lipman, who led the Universal label Republic Records. As she later explained, they told her, "Whatever you turn in, we will be proud to put out."[7] They told Swift that she would own the masters for albums recorded with their label, which was just as

Swift ended her working relationship with Big Machine and Scott Borchetta, *left*, in 2018 to work with Universal Music Group's Lucian Grainge, *right*, whom Swift said she shared a mutual trust.

important to her as choosing her own songs. Pleased with the deal, she split with Big Machine and signed on to Republic Records.

LOVER

Swift's first album with Republic was *Lover*, a definite departure from the moodier sound of many of the songs on *reputation*. Released on August 23, 2019, *Lover* had a softer, dreamier pop sound that grew out of her warm feelings about her relationship with Alwyn. She told *Vogue* magazine the album was a tribute to all the feelings that go along with new love.

Lover featured an array of love songs, including "ME!," "Lover," and "Cornelia Street." But the standout was "You Need to Calm Down," a song in which Swift championed the rights of the LGBTQ+ community. In addition to attacking homophobia, the song also condemned the way society often pits successful women against one another. In reference to that idea, Swift asked Perry to appear with her in the video, thus ending one of Swift's most enduring public feuds.

TAYLOR'S VERSIONS

While doing press for *Lover*, Swift made an important announcement about her future. It was about a June 2019 deal in which Big Machine sold the masters of Swift's

A VIDEO FULL OF STARS

The busy, candy-colored video of "You Need to Calm Down," set in a fanciful trailer park, gave fans plenty to look at. But on their initial viewings, many struggled to spot the more than two dozen celebrities featured in the video. They included former talk show host Ellen DeGeneres getting a tattoo, Olympic figure skater Adam Rippon selling snow cones, singer Ciara officiating a same-sex wedding, and YouTube star Hannah Hart weightlifting a boombox.

music to Scott "Scooter" Braun, a record executive who had once managed West's career. She was furious about the sale and wrote on social media, "Any time Scott Borchetta has heard the words 'Scooter Braun' escape my lips, it was when I was either crying or trying not to."[8]

At first, Swift thought there was nothing she could do. Then her friend singer Kelly Clarkson made a suggestion. Because Swift owned the composition rights to all her songs, she could rerecord her old albums and legally own the masters of the rerecordings. Her fans would want to buy her new versions to support her, especially if she sweetened the deal by adding old songs that had been dropped from her original albums.

It sounded like a questionable idea to spend so much time revisiting her old catalog. That time could be devoted to producing new music. But Swift was determined to own the masters of all her work, and her father assured her it made good business sense.

On August 22, 2019, she announced on *Good Morning America* that she would be recording her own version—Taylor's Version—of her first six albums. Work would begin after November 2020, when she would be released from her contract. She explained, "I think it's important for artists to own their work. . . . I'm gonna be busy."[9]

CHAPTER EIGHT

A CREATIVE QUARANTINE

A few months after the release of *Lover*, Taylor Swift was on the red carpet for the New York premiere of her latest movie, *Cats*. It was an adaptation of a long-running Broadway musical from the 1980s. In this show, all the actors play cat characters prowling through the streets of London.

Swift had eagerly signed on to play Bombalurina. After being lowered from the sky on a golden crescent moon, her character sings the sultry song "Macavity: The Mystery Cat" in a British accent. As she explained, "I have cats. I'm obsessed with them. I love my cats so much that when a role came up in a movie called *Cats*, I just thought, like, I gotta do this."[1]

Her role in *Cats* gave Swift an opportunity to act with stars such as Judi Dench, James Corden, and Jennifer Hudson. >>

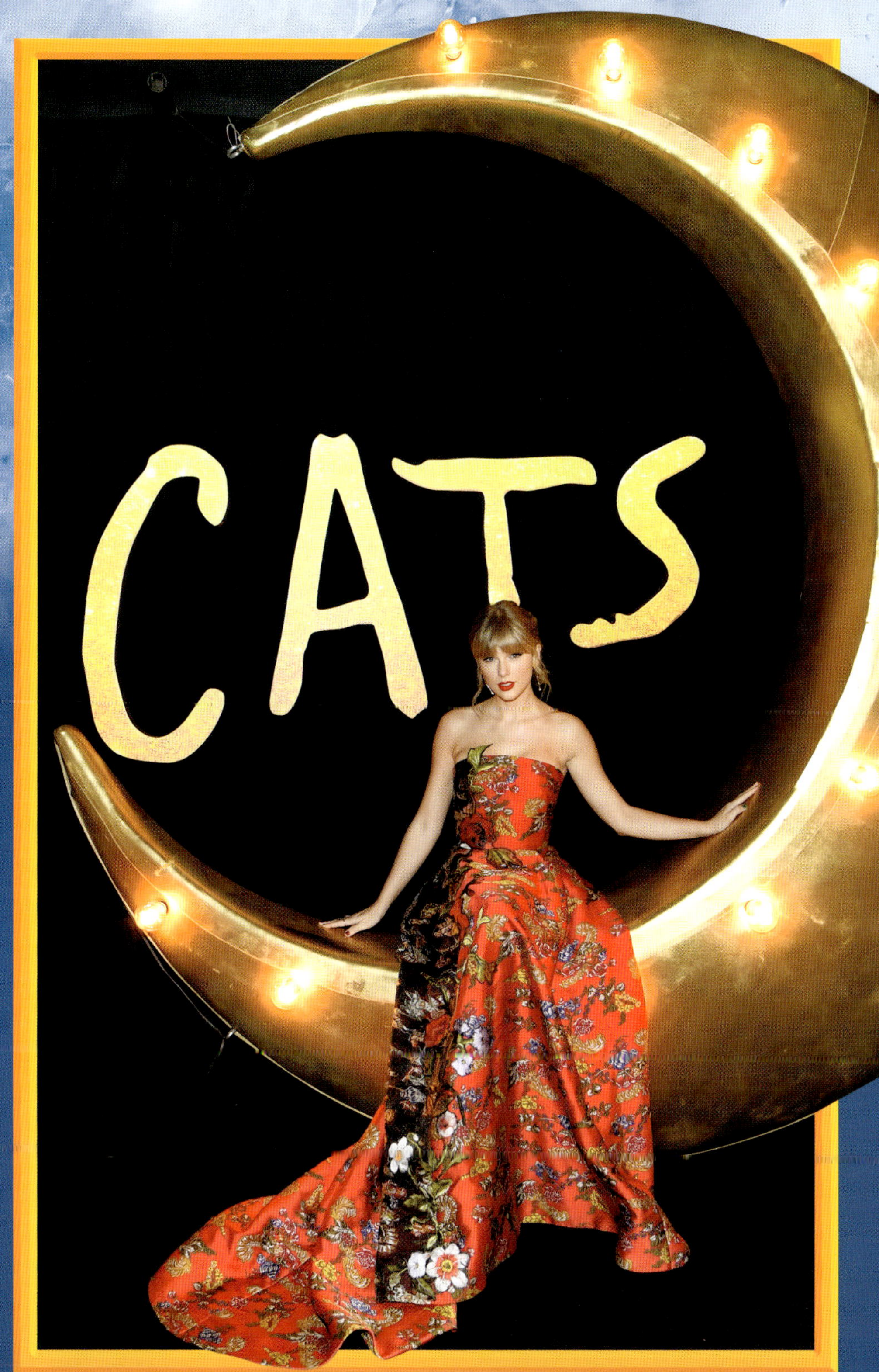
CATS

Cats bombed at the box office and didn't impress critics, who called it confusing and disjointed. But Swift had no regrets. She was excited to provide lyrics for a new song for the movie called "Beautiful Ghosts," which she wrote with theater legend Andrew Lloyd Webber. The song was nominated for a Golden Globe Award for Best Original Song.

SWIFT'S CATS

A proud self-avowed "cat lady," Swift travels with her three cats and often shares photographs and videos of them on social media. She named her first two cats after television characters—Meredith Grey on *Grey's Anatomy* and Olivia Benson on *Law & Order: SVU*. The two cats appeared in Swift's video for "ME!" On the set, Swift met and adopted a cat actor. Named after the title character in the movie *The Curious Case of Benjamin Button*, Benjamin the cat posed with Swift on the cover of *Time* magazine in 2023.

Swift's next film project, *Miss Americana*, premiered on the streaming service Netflix on January 31, 2020. The documentary covered Swift's life and career from the end of the *reputation* era to her crafting the songs that would appear on *Lover*. In the film, Swift talks about the difficulty of maturing from a girl to a woman in the public eye. She also reflects on the toll of constantly changing her image to maintain her audience's interest.

As she observes, "The female artists I know of have reinvented themselves 20 times more than the male artists. They have to or else they're out of a job." Throughout the documentary, Swift discusses her fear that she will soon be too old for the public to accept her as a pop star. Speaking of the release of *Lover*, she tells the camera, "This is probably one of my last opportunities as an artist to grasp on to that kind of success."[2]

FIGHTING DISORDERED EATING

In the documentary *Miss Americana*, Swift opened up about her past struggle with disordered eating. She explained that several times after seeing a photograph of herself "where I feel like I looked like my tummy was too big," her reaction was to stop eating altogether. *Miss Americana*'s director, Lana Wilson, praised Swift for speaking out: "I think it's really brave to see someone who is a role model for so many girls and women be really honest about [an eating disorder]. I think it will have a huge impact."[3]

CREATING CHARACTERS

Swift was preparing for her Lover Fest Tour when, in March 2020, the world shut down to contain the spread of the disease COVID-19. All over the United States, businesses closed and people confined themselves to their homes. Her tour postponed indefinitely, Swift holed up with Alwyn. As she waited out the pandemic, making new music about her life was far from her mind.

To pass the time, she and Alwyn got in the habit of watching a different movie each night, including such

Classic movies such as *Rear Window*, a 1954 film by Alfred Hitchcock starring James Stewart and Grace Kelly, provided inspiration for characters Swift wrote about in her songs.

classics as *Rear Window*, *Jane Eyre*, and *Pan's Labyrinth*. The films got her thinking in a new way. As she later explained, "I feel like consuming other people's art and storytelling sort of opened this portal in my imagination." Throughout her career, she had relied on her own experiences and feelings to provide the subject matter for her songwriting. Now she asked herself, "Why have I never created characters and intersecting story lines?"[4]

She began to write songs from the perspective of characters she made up. She let her imagination lead her songwriting. She focused on stories she wanted to tell.

One of those stories was a love triangle told through three songs, each from one of the lovers' points of view. The songs became "cardigan," "august," and "betty." She was particularly nervous about "betty" because it was written from the perspective of a 17-year-old boy.

Alwyn helped with the lyrics and is credited as William Bowery. Alwyn recalled, "It came about from messing around on a piano, and singing badly, then being overheard, and being like, 'Let's see what happens if we get to the end of it together.'"[5]

Swift still wrote songs about her own life, however. One of her lockdown songs, "my tears ricochet," was inspired by the 2019 movie *Marriage Story*, which told of a married couple's breakup. But it was also a way of processing her feelings of betrayal toward Borchetta of Big Machine Records after he refused to give her control of the masters of her early albums.

FOLKLORE AND EVERMORE

To record her new music, Swift turned to Jack Antonoff, one of her favorite collaborators. She also teamed up with Aaron Dessner from the indie rock band The National. Working remotely, they began laying down tracks, crafting a folk-rock sound for her latest songs. Swift gave her fans just one day's notice before releasing *folklore* on July 24, 2020. She regarded the album as "this really sweet, nice, pure part of the world as everything else in the world was burning and crashing and feeling this sickness and sadness."[6]

The public quickly embraced what felt like a surprise gift from Swift. Its soothing, soft acoustic sound reflected the loneliness and isolation people were feeling all around the world. Her fans enjoyed her new stripped-down sound, while she also gained the admiration of those who love indie rock. *Folklore* earned some of the best critical reviews of Swift's career and became the biggest selling album of 2020.

Swift has noted that after finishing an album, she usually wants to pivot in a new direction. But following the release of *folklore*, she had the rare urge to continue making music in the same vein. Released without fanfare just six months after *folklore*, its companion album *evermore* had many narrative songs.

These included "champagne problems," written with Alwyn about a failed marriage proposal, and "no body, no crime," a recounting of multiple murders inspired by Swift's love of true-crime podcasts. Swift worked with the band HAIM on the song. Other featured guests on *evermore* included Dessner's band The National on "coney island" and Bon Iver on the title song.

Folklore won a Grammy for Album of the Year in 2021, and *evermore* was nominated for the same award in 2022. In her acceptance speech for *folklore*, Swift thanked her

Swift accepted the Album of the Year Grammy for *folklore* with collaborators Laura Sisk, *left*, Jack Antonoff, Jonathan Low, and Aaron Dessner, *middle to right*.

fans, saying, "You guys met us in this imaginary world that we created, and we can't tell you how honored we are forever by this."[7] With the award, Swift joined Frank Sinatra, Stevie Wonder, and Paul Simon as the only artists to win Album of the Year three times.

A BUSY YEAR

In 2021, Swift began her project of rerecording her first six albums. The first Taylor's Version of a past album was *Fearless*, which was released in April 2021. Following the model she would subsequently use for all the rerecordings, *Fearless (Taylor's Version)* included "from the vault" songs that had been recorded but never previously released. Taylor's Versions gave her

Swift's *Red (Taylor's Version)* won Favorite Pop Album at the American Music Awards in Los Angeles, California, on November 20, 2022.

control of her earlier albums but were also a potential financial windfall. *Fearless (Taylor's Version)* skyrocketed to No. 1 on the *Billboard* 200 album chart, a first for a rerecorded album.

Released in November 2021, *Red (Taylor's Version)* was also a huge success. Its sales were bolstered by a new ten-minute version of the fan favorite "All Too Well," which became the longest song ever to top the singles chart. Swift wrote and directed the video for the song, which starred Sadie Sink and Dylan O'Brien. It won the Video of the Year and Best Direction awards at the 2022 VMAs and Best Music Video at the 2023 Grammys.

Swift was also busy creating new music for her album *Midnights*, which was released on October 21, 2022.

Described by Swift as "the story of 13 sleepless nights scattered throughout my life," *Midnights* marked a return to exploring intimate emotions through a synth pop style.[8] Swift collaborated closely with Antonoff on the 13 tracks, which included the song "Anti-Hero." Named by Swift as one of her favorite songs she has ever written, "Anti-Hero" is an unflinching examination of her personal flaws and insecurities.

Other singles included the disco-infused "Lavender Haze" and the catchy "Karma," while the introspective "You're on Your Own, Kid" appeared as track five. The release of *Midnights* along with the Taylor's Versions of *Fearless* and *Red* provided Swift's fans with the perfect entry point into her next phase, in which she would weave everything old and new together to create a spectacular and lucrative retrospective of her entire career.

CELEBRATING CAROLE KING

Taylor Swift opened the 2021 induction ceremony into the Rock and Roll Hall of Fame with a synth pop rendition of "Will You Still Love Me Tomorrow." The song is from *Tapestry*, the groundbreaking 1971 album by singer-songwriter Carole King. In her speech inducting King into the Hall of Fame, Swift recalled how her parents taught her to love King's music as a little girl. Swift also said, "Carole taught artists like me that telling your own story is worth the work and struggle it takes to win the opportunity for your story to be heard."[9]

CHAPTER NINE

THE BIGGEST STAR IN THE WORLD

On November 1, 2022, the hosts of *Good Morning America* explained that Taylor Swift had become the first artist in history to hold all of the top ten spots on the *Billboard* Hot 100, with every spot filled by a song from *Midnights*. The album's lead single, "Anti-Hero" was her 40th No. 1 hit. The hosts then introduced Swift, who appeared on video to announce her first tour in five years. She promised the Eras Tour would include music from every one of her musical eras.

Tickets for the Eras Tour went on sale on November 15. Millions of fans flooded the Ticketmaster website, causing it to crash. Frustrated Swifties had

During the Eras Tour, Swift marked each era with a wardrobe change, wearing this purple Oscar de la Renta dress during her *Midnights* set. >>

QUILL, FOUNTAIN, AND GLITTER

Swift once revealed that she places songs from all her eras into three broad categories based on the writing tool she imagines herself holding while composing them. Her Quill songs use words and phrases that seem to come from a bygone time. She gave the example of "ivy" from *evermore*. Fountain Pen songs are about a contemporary moment but with a poetic twist, such as *Red's* "All Too Well." Glitter Gel Pen songs are bouncy and frivolous, such as "You Belong With Me" from her *fearless* album.

to wait hours to purchase tickets, which sold out quickly. On websites that allowed people to resell tickets, those in front of the stage were priced as high as $21,600.[1] Given the public's intense desire to see the show, it was quickly clear that the Eras Tour was poised to be a major event in American culture.

OPENING NIGHT

After months of frenzied anticipation, the first Swift fans finally got their chance to see the Eras Tour when it premiered in Glendale, Arizona, on March 17, 2023. Just before showtime, the crowd cheered as a timer was projected on a massive screen onstage that counted down the three minutes before the concert was to begin. Then Swift appeared onstage, wearing a pink-and-blue body suit and knee-high boots.

Swift opened with a set of songs from her album *Lover*. This was a nod to the Lover Fest Tour she had to cancel

On the Eras Tour, Swift crossed five continents, performing 149 shows in 51 cities over a span of nearly two years.

because of the early pandemic. Lights bathed the stage in cotton-candy pink, and a glowing dollhouse appeared on the screen, recalling images from the video for the song "Lover."

A few songs in, Swift told the audience, "So tonight, we're going to go through an adventure, one era at a time."[2] The concert then moved from one album to the next. The set design, lighting, props, and costumes created an entirely new look and feel for each era.

For *Red*, Swift wore the iconic oversized T-shirt and black hat from her video for "22" as her backup dancers

Swifties worldwide showed up to the Eras Tour shows in sequined dresses and cowboy boots, ready to exchange friendship bracelets with other fans.

were all dressed in red. For *Speak Now*, Swift donned a glittering princess ball gown as a field of purple flowers was digitally projected on the stage and screen. For *reputation*, Swift appeared in a one-legged black catsuit embroidered with snakes and sang before a wall of glass boxes, in which her dancers performed in outfits associated with earlier incarnations of Swift.

For sister albums *folklore* and *evermore*, the stage was filled with a forest cabin lit with candles, and Swift sat at a moss-covered piano in a flowing gown. For *Midnights*, dark lights created a nighttime ambience echoed by her sparkling midnight blue minidress. And for the finale, Swift turned the entire stadium into a dance party as she and her fans belted out the lively chorus to "Karma."

A CRITICAL AND FINANCIAL SUCCESS

Critics' reviews of the show were ecstatic. *Rolling Stone* said, "The Eras Tour is a feat. It's live music at its highest spectacle and greatest excess."[3] *The Atlantic* wrote, "The concert had been unbelievable, but so was the fact that this one human woman planned to do it again the next night and for many after."[4]

Fans were just as enthusiastic, enjoying not just the show but also the experience of sharing it with a crowd of other Swifties. By dressing up as their favorite version of Swift and exchanging friendship bracelets, they developed a sense of community, which was especially welcome coming on the heels of the COVID-19 lockdown. Swift's long career also meant that attending the Eras Tour shows was often a multigenerational experience, allowing parents and teens to bond over the fact that they had both grown up with Swift's music.

The tour also provided an economic boon to the cities and towns in which Swift performed. The average attendee spent about $1,300 on travel, lodging, food, and merchandise.[5] This rise in tourism dollars wherever she played was nicknamed the "Taylor effect."

Swift added to the Taylor effect by donating money to local food banks in every city she performed. She also shared a portion of her profits from the successful tour

THE SWIFT QUAKE

Eras Tour concerts held at Lumen Field in Seattle, Washington, were literally earthshaking. During the show, thousands of fans sang, danced, and jumped around so enthusiastically that they caused significant seismic activity. The earth shook as much as it would during a 2.3 magnitude earthquake.[6] Appropriately, researchers found that one of the songs that caused the most shaking was Swift's 2014 hit "Shake It Off."

with everyone who worked on it, including dancers, band members, carpenters, security guards, and truck drivers. By the tour's end, she had paid out $197 million in bonuses on top of tour workers' regular salaries.[7]

NEW ROMANCES

Although the Eras Tour was an enormous success from the start, in its early months Swift was suffering from personal turmoil. Just as the tour began, she and Alwyn broke up after dating for more than six years. About a month later, she began seeing Matty Healy, the lead singer of the British rock band The 1975.

During their brief romance, some fans called on Swift to break things off, citing that Healy earlier in the year had laughed at some racist jokes on a podcast. Fans feared the relationship could tarnish her reputation. After a few weeks, the couple broke up.

Friends and family alerted Swift to another podcast, *New Heights with Jason & Travis Kelce.* The show was hosted by a pair of brothers who were both professional football players. On one episode, Travis Kelce said he had attended an Eras Tour concert in hopes of meeting Swift after the show and giving her a friendship bracelet with his phone number on it.

Swift celebrated with boyfriend Travis Kelce after the Kansas City Chiefs defeated the Buffalo Bills on January 26, 2025.

Charmed by the story, Swift contacted Kelce and the two began seeing each other. They made their relationship public on September 24, 2023, when Swift attended a Kansas City Chiefs game with Kelce's mother. Her continued presence at Chiefs games increased the female television viewership of their games by 9 percent.[8] Swift was new to football, but she quickly became a fan.

NEW RECORDINGS

Swift released Taylor's Versions of *Speak Now* in July 2023 and *1989* in October 2023 to widespread acclaim and impressive sales. With 1.36 million copies sold in the first week, *1989 (Taylor's Version)* became the first rerecording ever to outsell the original.[9] On February 4, 2024, when Swift won the Grammy Award for Best Pop Vocal Album for *Midnights*, she announced in her acceptance speech that her eleventh studio album, *The Tortured Poets Department*, would go on sale in April.

> **"There is one thing I've learned: My response to anything that happens, good or bad, is to keep making things. Keep making art."**[10]
>
> **—Swift, 2023**

Released while her Eras Tour was still in full swing, *The Tortured Poets Department* spent 15 weeks at the top of the *Billboard* 200 chart. The 31-track double album sounded similar to *Midnights* and *Lover*, and many songs examined romantic heartbreak and confusion. The melancholy "So Long, London" was probably a reflection on her breakup with Alwyn, while "The Alchemy," thought to be about Kelce, explored the excitement of new love. Her relationship with Healy came under scrutiny as well in songs such as "Fortnight," which was nominated for Song of the Year and Record of the Year at the 2025 Grammys.

OWNING THE MASTERS

Swift received some of the best news of her career in May 2025. After a 20-year court battle with Big Machine, Swift was finally able to buy back the rights to all the masters of her music. This means she has full control over how her music is used and licensed going forward. Swift was over the moon about the news. "To say this is my greatest dream come true is actually being pretty reserved about it."[13] She thanked fans for their show of support throughout the long ordeal.

THE GREATEST AWARD

On December 8, 2024, Swift performed her final concert of the Eras Tour in the Canadian city of Vancouver. Five days later, she turned 35, having spent more than half of her life in the spotlight. The Eras Tour had taken her to heights few performers had ever known. More than just an international pop star, Swift was now a cultural phenomenon.

She was also one of the richest. The Eras Tour was the most financially successful tour of all time, grossing more than $2 billion.[11] Swift's share of the profits had brought her net worth to an estimated $1.6 billion.[12]

Swift had also won a place in the pantheon of popular entertainment. As one of the top ten best-selling artists of all time, she joined such revered performers as Michael Jackson, Elvis Presley, and Madonna. From her peers, she had also received virtually every award possible, including 58 Grammy nominations and 14 wins.

By April 2025, at least 129,000 copies of Swift's *Midnights* had sold on vinyl alone, making it the top-selling record of the decade.

One of those wins was the 2024 Album of the Year Grammy for *Midnights*, which made Swift the only artist in history to receive that honor four times. In her speech, she said, "I would love to tell you that this is the best moment of my life." But she admitted she could not, because she felt the same happiness every time she finished a song. "The award is the work," she declared, adding, "All I want to do is to keep being able to do this."[14] This sentiment is shared by millions of fans who look forward to many new eras for Taylor Swift in the decades to come.

The next era began with a bang. On August 13, 2025, Swift announced the release of her twelfth studio album, *The Life of a Showgirl*. Then on August 26, Swift and Kelce posted news of their engagement on Instagram. Fans were thrilled for the couple.

ESSENTIAL FACTS

Full Name: Taylor Alison Swift

Date of Birth: December 13, 1989

Place of Birth: West Reading, Pennsylvania

Parents: Scott and Andrea Swift

Education: Hendersonville High School, Aaron Academy

RISE TO STARDOM

- When Taylor Swift was 14, she signed a development contract with Sony/ATV.
- After performing at a talent showcase, 16-year-old Swift landed a recording contract with Big Machine Records.
- Her first album, *Taylor Swift* was released by Big Machine Records in 2006.
- In 2007, Swift won the Horizon Award from the Country Music Association.

CAREER HIGHLIGHTS

- In 2021, Swift began rerecording her first six albums, calling them Taylor's Versions, in order to control the rights to master recordings of her early work.
- In 2023 and 2024, her Eras Tour became the first tour to gross more than $2 billion.
- *Time* magazine named Taylor Swift its Person of the Year for 2023.

- In February 2024, Swift won her fourth Grammy for Album of the Year for *Midnights*. Her earlier wins were for *Fearless*, *1989*, and *folklore*.
- By early 2025, Taylor Swift had released 11 original studio albums and won 14 Grammys.
- In May 2025, Swift bought back the rights to her Big Machine recordings.

MAJOR ALBUMS

- *Fearless* (2008)
- *Red* (2012)
- *1989* (2014)
- *reputation* (2017)
- *folklore* (2020)

QUOTE

"I can't even believe this is real. This is definitely the highlight of my senior year."

—Taylor Swift accepting the Horizon Award for best new artist at the 2007 Country Music Association Awards

GLOSSARY

backlash

An angry response to something or someone.

catalog

A collection of musical compositions owned by a company or a person.

debut

The first release of a product, such as a song or an album, by a musician or artist.

demo

An unpolished recording used to show the potential of a song or a singer.

disordered eating

Harmful eating habits that include restricting eating, eating compulsively, or eating irregularly.

extended play (EP)

A musical recording that usually includes four to six songs.

gaslit

Made a person doubt their judgment or understanding of a situation, in a form of psychological abuse.

genre

A distinct style of musical, literary, or artistic work.

gross

To earn income.

headliner
The main performer on a musical tour or at a musical event.

label
A company that produces and distributes musical recordings.

liner notes
The descriptive text found on the sleeve of a physical music album.

master
The original recording of a song or an album, from which all copies are made.

pandemic
An outbreak of disease over a large area.

quarantine
A state or period of isolation, often to prevent the spread of a disease.

synth pop
A style of popular music that makes heavy use of an electronic musical instrument called a synthesizer.

trademark
The legal registration of a word or a symbol so that it can be used only by its owner.

ADDITIONAL RESOURCES

SELECTED BIBLIOGRAPHY

Dailey, Hannah. "*Billboard*'s Greatest Pop Stars of the 21st Century: No. 2—Taylor Swift." *Billboard*, 26 Nov. 2024, billboard.com. Accessed 18 Mar. 2025.

Evers, Kevin. "The Strategic Genius of Taylor Swift." *Harvard Business Review*, Mar./Apr. 2025, hbr.org. Accessed 18 Mar. 2025.

Lansky, Sam. "Taylor Swift, 2023 TIME Person of the Year." *Time*, 6 Dec. 2023, time.com. Accessed 11 Mar. 2025.

FURTHER READINGS

Chapelle, Sarah. *Taylor Swift Style: Fashion Through the Eras*. St. Martin's Griffin, 2024.

Corbett, Holly C., et al. *Taylor Swift*. Hearst Home, 2024.

McCausland, Elly. *Stars around My Scars: The Annotated Poetry of Taylor Swift*. Andrews McNeel, 2025.

ONLINE RESOURCES

To learn more about Taylor Swift, please visit **abdobooklinks.com** or scan this QR code. These links are routinely monitored and updated to provide the most current information available.

MORE INFORMATION

For more information on this subject, contact or visit the following organizations:

THE BLUEBIRD CAFE

4104 Hillsboro Pike
Nashville, TN 37215
bluebirdcafe.com

Taylor Swift signed her first record deal after performing in a talent showcase at this revered music venue. The Bluebird features nightly shows highlighting established and up-and-coming singer-songwriters.

OHEKA CASTLE

135 W. Gate Dr.
Huntington, NY 11743
oheka.com

Taylor Swift's video for "Blank Space" was filmed at the Oheka Castle, which is now a hotel. The historic site offers daily guided tours of portions of the building and its grounds.

TAYLOR SWIFT EDUCATION CENTER

Country Music Hall of Fame and Museum
222 Rep. John Lewis Way S.
Nashville, TN 27303
countrymusichalloffame.org/learn/taylor-swift-education-center

Funded by Taylor Swift, this educational center offers programs about the history and culture of country music. The museum also has on display a purple gown Swift wore during the *Speak Now* section of the Eras Tour.

SOURCE NOTES

CHAPTER 1. EVERYTHING FOR THE FANS

1. Tony Cabrera. "Taylor Swift Makes Surprise Announcement Just Before LA Premiere of 'Eras Tour' Film at the Grove." *KABC*, 11 Oct. 2023, abc7.com. Accessed 25 Mar. 2025.

2. Rachel Treisman. "The Eras Era Ends: A Look Back at Taylor Swift's Record-Breaking, 21-Month Tour." *National Public Radio*, 9 Dec. 2024, npr.org. Accessed 25 Aug. 2025.

3. Cabrera, "Taylor Swift Makes Surprise Announcement."

4. Emily Yahr and Michael Cavna. "With 'The Eras Tour,' Taylor Swift's Empire Conquers the Movie Industry." *Washington Post*, 11 Oct. 2023, washingtonpost.com. Accessed 25 Mar. 2025.

5. Natalie Sitek and Anthony D'Alessandro. "Taylor Swift Calls Fans 'Main Characters' in 'Eras Tour' Concert Film." *Deadline*, 11 Oct. 2023, deadline.com. Accessed 25 Mar. 2025.

6. Kirsten Chuba. "Taylor Swift's 'Eras Tour' Premiere." *Hollywood Reporter*, 11 Oct. 2023, hollywoodreporter.com. Accessed 25 Mar. 2025.

7. Sitek and D'Alessandro, "Taylor Swift Calls Fans 'Main Characters.'"

8. Julius Miller. "'13 Out of 10:' Swifties Review 'Eras Tour' Movie." *Los Angeles Magazine*, 12 Oct. 2023, lamag.com. Accessed 25 Mar. 2025.

CHAPTER 2. DREAMING OF A MUSIC CAREER

1. Holly C. Corbett et al. *Taylor Swift*. Hearst Home, 2024. 90.

2. Rob Sheffield. *Heartbreak Is the National Anthem: How Taylor Swift Reinvented Pop Music*. Dey Street Books, 2024. 26.

3. Corbett et al., *Taylor Swift*, 88.

4. Corbett et al., *Taylor Swift*, 44.

5. Corbett et al., *Taylor Swift*, 92.

6. Annie Zaleski. *Taylor Swift: The Stories Behind the Songs*. Welbeck, 2024. 23.

7. Corbett et al., *Taylor Swift*, 50.

CHAPTER 3. A STAR IS BORN

1. Kevin Evers. "The Strategic Genius of Taylor Swift." *Harvard Business Review*, Mar./Apr. 2025, hbr.org. Accessed 18 Mar. 2025.

2. Annie Zaleski. *Taylor Swift: The Stories Behind the Songs*. Welbeck, 2024. 11.

3. "Taylor Swift—Tim McGraw (Academy of Country Music Awards (ACMs), 2007)." *YouTube*, uploaded by Taylor Swift Evolution, 26 Oct. 2021, youtube.com. Accessed 5 April 2025.

4. Holly C. Corbett et al. *Taylor Swift*. Hearst Home, 2024. 43.

5. Corbett et al., *Taylor Swift*, 45.

6. Zaleski, *Taylor Swift*, 71.

7. Mary Perez. "Taylor Swift Once Headlined a Concert in Biloxi." *SunHerald*, 3 Aug. 2023, sunherald.com. Accessed 10 July 2025.

8. "Taylor Swift Album Goes Triple Platinum." *ABC News*, 29 Apr. 2008, abcnews.go.com. Accessed 10 July 2025.

CHAPTER 4. TAKING CONTROL

1. Daniel Kreps. "Kanye West Storms the VMAs Stage." *Rolling Stone*, 13 Sept. 2009, rollingstone.com. Accessed 10 Apr. 2025.

2. Holly C. Corbett et al. *Taylor Swift*. Hearst Home, 2024. 69.

3. Chuck Klosterman. "Taylor Swift's Realest Interview Ever." *GQ*, 15 Oct. 2015, gq.com. Accessed 16 Mar. 2025.

4. Bob Lefsetz. "Grammys." *Lefsetz Report*, n.d., lefsetz.com. Accessed 9 Apr. 2025.

5. "Taylor Swift—#VEVOCertified, Pt. 3: Taylor Talks About Her Fans." *YouTube*, uploaded by Taylor Swift, 29 Oct. 2012, youtube.com. Accessed 13 Apr. 2025.

6. Jody Rosen. "Why Taylor Swift Is the Reigning Queen of Pop." *Vulture*, 17 Nov. 2013, vulture.com. Accessed 15 Mar. 2025.

CHAPTER 5. *1989*

1. Mary Kate Carr. "A Golden Globe Joke Has Altered Taylor Swift's Career." *AV Club*, 9 Jan. 2024, avclub.com. Accessed 12 Apr. 2025.

2. Abby Aguirre. "Taylor Swift on Sexism, Scrutiny, and Standing Up for Herself." *Vogue*, 8 Aug. 2019, vogue.com. Accessed 15 Mar. 2025.

3. Nancy Jo Sales. "Taylor Swift's Telltale Heart." *Vanity Fair*, Apr. 2023, vanityfair.com. Accessed 15 Mar. 2025.

4. Jody Rosen. "Why Taylor Swift Is the Reigning Queen of Pop." *Vulture*, 17 Nov. 2013, vulture.com. Accessed 15 Mar. 2025.

5. Rosen, "Why Taylor Swift Is the Reigning Queen of Pop."

6. Raisa Bruner. "How 1989 Changed Taylor Swift's Career Forever." *Time*, 26 Oct. 2023, time.com. Accessed 14 Apr. 2025.

7. Chuck Klosterman. "Taylor Swift's Realest Interview Ever." *GQ*, 15 Oct. 2015, gq.com. Accessed 16 Mar. 2025.

8. Holly C. Corbett et al. *Taylor Swift*. Hearst Home, 2024. 96.

9. Corbett et al., *Taylor Swift*, 27.

10. "'Anything that Connects': A Conversation with Taylor Swift." *NPR*, 31 Oct. 2014, npr.com. Accessed 16 Mar. 2025.

CHAPTER 6. FIGHTING BACK

1. "Grammys: Taylor Swift Fires Back at Kanye West." *Hollywood Reporter*, 16 Feb. 2016, hollywoodreporter.com. Accessed 15 Apr. 2025.

2. "Grammys: Taylor Swift Fires Back."

3. Chuck Klosterman. "Taylor Swift's Realest Interview Ever." *GQ*, 15 Oct. 2015, gq.com. Accessed 16 Mar. 2025.

4. Klosterman, "Taylor Swift's Realest Interview Ever."

5. Constance Grady. "Newly Leaked Footage Shows Taylor Swift and Kanye West Talking 'Famous.'" *Vox*, 21 March 2020, vox.com. Accessed 15 Apr. 2025.

6. Abby Aguirre. "Taylor Swift on Sexism, Scrutiny, and Standing Up for Herself." *Vogue*, 8 Aug. 2019, vogue.com. Accessed 15 Mar. 2025.

SOURCE NOTES

7. Grady, "Swift and West Talking 'Famous.'"

8. Eliana Dockterman. "Taylor Swift on What Powered Her Sexual Assault Testimony." *Time*, 6 Dec. 2017, time.com. Accessed 15 Apr. 2025.

9. Taylor Swift. *Miss Americana*. Directed by Lana Wilson, 2020. Netflix, netflix.com.

CHAPTER 7. BOLDER THAN EVER

1. Mark Harris. "Taylor Swift's 'Look What You Made Me Do' Is the First Pure Piece of Trump-Era Pop Art." *Vulture*, 30 Aug. 2017, vulture.com. Accessed 15 Apr. 2025.

2. Constance Grady. "A Unified Theory of Taylor Swift's Reputation." *Vox*, 7 May 2018, vox.com. Accessed 17 Mar. 2025.

3. Annie Zaleski. *Taylor Swift: The Stories Behind the Songs*. Welbeck, 2024. 287.

4. Holly C. Corbett et al. *Taylor Swift*. Hearst Home, 2024. 16.

5. Taylor Swift. *Miss Americana*. Directed by Lana Wilson, 2020. Netflix, netflix.com.

6. Samantha Olson. "A Definitive Ranking of Taylor Swift's Track 5 Songs." *Cosmopolitan*, 22 Apr. 2024, cosmopolitan.com. Accessed 18 Apr. 2025.

7. Sam Lansky. "Taylor Swift, 2023 TIME Person of the Year." *Time*, 6 Dec. 2023, time.com. Accessed 10 July 2025.

8. Alice Vincent. "Taylor Swift: The Rise, Fall and Re-invention of America's Sweetheart." *Telegraph*, 25 Jan. 2020, telegraph.co.uk. Accessed 17 Mar. 2025.

9. Michael Rothman. "Taylor Swift Performs Live on 'GMA.'" *Good Morning America*, 22 Aug. 2019, goodmorningamerica.com. Accessed 18 Apr. 2025.

CHAPTER 8. A CREATIVE QUARANTINE

1. Holly C. Corbett et al. *Taylor Swift*. Hearst Home, 2024. 109.

2. Taylor Swift. *Miss Americana*. Directed by Lana Wilson, 2020. Netflix, netflix.com.

3. Chris Willman. "Taylor Swift Opens Up about Overcoming Struggle with Eating Disorder (EXCLUSIVE)." *Variety*, 23 Jan. 2020, variety.com. Accessed 20 Apr. 2025.

4. Alex Suskind. "Taylor Swift Broke All Her Rules with Folklore." *Entertainment Weekly*, 8 Dec. 2020, ew.com. Accessed 19 Mar. 2025.

5. Corbett et al., *Taylor Swift*, 113.

6. Suskind, "Taylor Swift Broke All Her Rules with Folklore."

7. Heran Mamo. "Taylor Swift Wins Album of the Year for 'Folklore.'" *Billboard*, 14 Mar. 2021, billboard.com. Accessed 10 July 2025.

8. Michael Ray. "Taylor Swift." *Britannica*, 19 Mar. 2025, britannica.com. Accessed 19 Mar. 2025.

9. "Taylor Swift Inducts Carole King into the Hall of Fame." *YouTube*, uploaded by SOL Music Fan, 20 Nov. 2021, youtube.com. Accessed 20 Apr. 2025.

CONTINUED. . .

CHAPTER 9. THE BIGGEST STAR IN THE WORLD

1. Frank Pallotta. "Taylor Swift Tickets Listed for Thousands on StubHub." *CNN Business*, 16 Nov. 2022, cnn.com. Accessed 22 Apr. 2025.

2. Waiss Aramesh. "Taylor Swift's The Eras Tour Is a 3-Hour Career-Spanning Victory Lap." *Rolling Stone*, 18 Mar. 2023, rollingstone.com. Accessed 22 Mar. 2025.

3. Aramesh, "Taylor Swift's The Eras Tour."

4. Constance Grady. "The Eras Concert Movie Is Taylor Swift Leveling Up." *Vox*, 12 Oct. 2023, vox.com. Accessed 17 Mar. 2025.

5. Abha Bhattarai et al. "The Economy (Taylor's Version)." *Washington Post*, 13 Oct. 2023, washingtonpost.com. Accessed 10 July 2025.

6. Amanda Zhou. "Taylor Swift Sang 'Shake It Off' in Seattle." *Seattle Times*, 27 July 2023, seattletimes.com. Accessed 23 Apr. 2025.

7. Melody Chiu and Jeff Nelson. "Taylor Swift Gave a Whopping $197 Million in Bonuses to Eras Tour Performers, Crew." *People*, 9 Dec. 2024, people.com. Accessed 23 Apr. 2025.

8. Holly C. Corbett et al. *Taylor Swift*. Hearst Home, 2024. 141.

9. Hannah Dailey. "Billboard's Greatest Pop Stars of the 21st Century: No. 2—Taylor Swift." *Billboard*, 26 Nov. 2024, billboard.com. Accessed 18 Mar. 2025.

10. Sam Lansky. "Taylor Swift, 2023 TIME Person of the Year." *Time*, 6 Dec. 2023, time.com. Accessed 25 Apr. 2025.

11. Ben Sisario. "Taylor Swift's Eras Tour Grand Total: A Record $2 Billion." *New York Times*, 9 Dec. 2024, nytimes.com. Accessed 25 Apr. 2025.

12. Kevin Evers. "The Strategic Genius of Taylor Swift." *Harvard Business Review*, Mar./Apr. 2025, hbr.org. Accessed 18 Mar. 2025.

13. Mark Savage. "Taylor Swift Buys Back Her Master Recordings." *BBC*, 30 May 2025, bbc.com. Accessed 10 July 2025.

14. "Taylor Swift Wins Album of the Year for 'MIDNIGHTS'/2024 GRAMMYs Acceptance Speech." *YouTube*, uploaded by Recording Academy/Grammys, 4 Feb. 2024, youtube.com. Accessed 25 Apr. 2025.

INDEX

ABOUT THE AUTHOR

LIZ SONNEBORN

A graduate of Swarthmore College, Liz Sonneborn has written more than 120 books for young readers and adults on a wide variety of subjects. Her specialties include American history, world history, biography, women's studies, African American studies, and American pop culture. Sonneborn is a longtime resident of Brooklyn, New York.